Mental Health 101: Self-Care for the Modern Mind

By: Monica Lynne Chase

Foreword

In our increasingly fast-paced and demanding world, mental health often takes a backseat to the pressures of daily life. Many of us find ourselves juggling responsibilities, facing constant distractions, and struggling to maintain a sense of balance. It's easy to neglect our emotional well-being in the hustle, leading to stress, anxiety, and burnout. That's why Mental Health 101: Self-Care for the Modern Mind is such a vital resource for anyone looking to reclaim their mental health and cultivate a more fulfilling life.

This book offers practical tools and insights that empower you to recognize the signs of stress and anxiety while equipping you with effective strategies to combat them. Monica Lynne Chase combines her personal experiences with actionable advice, making mental health accessible and relatable. Through her thoughtful exploration of emotional intelligence and self-care techniques, she provides readers with a roadmap to better understand themselves and foster resilience.

As you journey through this book, remember that prioritizing your mental health is not a luxury but a necessity. By investing in self-care and building a support network, you are taking crucial steps toward a healthier, happier you. Embrace the practical tips and exercises within these pages, and allow them to guide you on your path to mental wellness. This is your time to cultivate a mindful approach to life and to nurture your most important asset: your mind.

Table of Contents

Chapter 1: Introduction to Emotional Intelligence

Understanding Emotional Intelligence

Emotional intelligence (EI) is a critical component of mental health and self-care that involves recognizing, understanding, and managing our emotions as well as the emotions of others. It encompasses a range of skills that contribute to effective communication, empathy, and interpersonal relationships. By developing emotional intelligence, individuals can enhance their awareness of emotional triggers, improve their coping strategies, and foster healthier connections with others. This foundation allows for a more profound engagement with self-care practices, enabling individuals to respond to stressors in a balanced and constructive manner.

The five key components of emotional intelligence include self-awareness, self-regulation, motivation, empathy, and social skills. Self-awareness is the ability to accurately recognize one's emotions and their impact on thoughts and behaviors. This awareness is crucial for personal growth and can be cultivated through techniques such as journaling and mindfulness meditation. By reflecting on daily experiences and emotions, individuals can identify patterns in their emotional responses, leading to greater insight and ultimately more intentional actions.

Self-regulation, the second component, involves managing one's emotions effectively, particularly in stressful situations. This skill can be developed through practices like mindfulness and deep-breathing exercises, which help individuals pause and reflect before reacting impulsively. By enhancing self-regulation, individuals can navigate challenging interactions and emotional upheavals with greater resilience, leading to healthier relationships and reduced stress levels.

Motivation, the third element of emotional intelligence, goes beyond intrinsic drive; it involves harnessing emotions to pursue goals with a positive attitude. Individuals who are emotionally intelligent tend to be more adaptable and open to change, which can be particularly beneficial in navigating life's challenges. Cultivating motivation can be achieved through setting achievable goals, celebrating small victories, and maintaining a positive mindset even in the face of adversity. These practices can significantly improve one's overall mental health and well-being.

Empathy and social skills are the final components of emotional intelligence that facilitate effective communication and relationship-building. Empathy allows individuals to connect with others on a deeper level, understanding their perspectives and emotions. This connection fosters supportive relationships, which are essential for mental health. Developing social skills through active listening and open communication can enhance one's ability to create a robust support system. Recognizing when to reach out for help and effectively utilizing available mental health resources are vital aspects of maintaining emotional health and well-being, ensuring that individuals are not navigating their challenges alone.

Regarding these elements, I may later take the opportunity to write pamphlets for each one individually as I navigate through the complexities of the world. It sometimes seems that these elements were either missed in class or perhaps were never taught at all, which could indicate a noticeable generational gap in understanding.

The Importance of Emotional Intelligence in Daily Life

Emotional intelligence (EI) plays a crucial role in our daily lives, influencing how we interact with others and manage our own emotions. At its core, EI involves the ability to recognize, understand, and regulate emotions—both in ourselves and in those around us. This skillset is essential for effective communication and building strong relationships, which are foundational to mental health. By cultivating emotional intelligence, individuals can navigate social complexities more adeptly, leading to healthier interactions and a greater sense of community.

In the context of self-care and mental health, emotional intelligence empowers individuals to recognize their emotional triggers and responses. For instance, when faced with stress, those with high EI can identify the emotions at play, whether it's anxiety, frustration, or sadness. This awareness allows for more thoughtful decision-making rather than reactive behavior. Techniques such as journaling can enhance this self-awareness by providing a space to reflect on daily emotions and events, ultimately facilitating a deeper understanding of one's emotional landscape.

Moreover, emotional intelligence is instrumental in practicing self-compassion. By recognizing that everyone experiences emotional ups and downs, individuals can cultivate a more forgiving and understanding attitude toward themselves. This shift in perspective not only alleviates self-criticism but also fosters resilience in the face of challenges. As individuals learn to treat themselves with kindness during difficult times, they are better equipped to extend that same compassion to others, creating a supportive environment that promotes mental well-being.

Understanding when and how to reach out for help is another vital aspect of emotional intelligence. Those with high EI are often more attuned to their own needs and the needs of others, making it easier to identify when additional support is necessary. Whether it involves seeking professional therapy, confiding in a friend, or accessing mental health resources, recognizing the importance of external support can be a transformative step in one's self-care journey. Emotional intelligence not only facilitates these connections but also enriches the quality of support received, as individuals can communicate their needs more effectively.

In summary, the importance of emotional intelligence in daily life cannot be overstated. It enhances interpersonal relationships, fosters self-awareness, encourages self-compassion, and facilitates the seeking of support. As individuals work to develop their emotional intelligence, they contribute not only to their own mental health but also to the well-being of those around them. By weaving emotional intelligence into the fabric of self-care practices, individuals can cultivate a more harmonious and fulfilling life, ultimately leading to greater resilience in the face of life's challenges.

The Role of Emotional Intelligence in Mental Health

Emotional intelligence (EI) plays a crucial role in mental health, serving as a foundation for understanding and managing our own emotions while also navigating interpersonal relationships. At its core, emotional intelligence involves the ability to recognize, understand, and influence one's own emotions and the emotions of others. This skill is particularly important in the context of self-care, as it allows individuals to identify emotional triggers and respond to them in a constructive manner. By developing emotional intelligence, people can enhance their resilience, cope more effectively with stress, and foster healthier relationships, all of which contribute to improved mental well-being.

One of the key components of emotional intelligence is self-awareness, which involves recognizing and understanding one's own emotional states. When individuals are self-aware, they can better articulate their feelings and thoughts, making it easier to engage in self-care practices such as journaling or meditation. These techniques can be instrumental in processing emotions, providing an outlet for reflection and helping to clarify thoughts. For example, through journaling, an individual may uncover underlying feelings of anxiety or sadness, prompting them to address these emotions before they escalate. This proactive approach can significantly mitigate the risk of mental health challenges.

In addition to self-awareness, emotional intelligence encompasses self-regulation, which is the ability to manage one's emotions in healthy ways. This skill is vital for stress management, as it enables individuals to respond to stressful situations with composure rather than allowing emotions to dictate their reactions. Techniques such as mindfulness and meditation can enhance self-regulation by fostering a calmer, more centered state of mind. By practicing these techniques, individuals learn to pause before reacting, allowing them to choose responses that are more aligned with their long-term mental health goals rather than immediate emotional impulses.

Empathy, another essential aspect of emotional intelligence, involves the ability to understand and share the feelings of others. Cultivating empathy can strengthen social connections and support systems, which are fundamental for mental health. When individuals are empathetic, they are more likely to seek help when needed and to offer support to others in their network. This reciprocal relationship can create a nurturing environment where open discussions about mental health are encouraged, reducing stigma and fostering a sense of community. Engaging in group activities, whether through support groups or social gatherings, can enhance feelings of connection and belonging.

Emotional intelligence empowers individuals to practice self-compassion, which is critical in the journey of self-care. Instead of being overly critical of oneself during challenging times, emotionally intelligent individuals can approach themselves with kindness and understanding. This attitude helps to combat negative self-talk and promotes a more positive self-image. Recognizing when to reach out for help and knowing how to access mental health resources becomes easier when individuals possess a strong sense of emotional intelligence. By embracing these skills, individuals can take proactive steps toward maintaining their mental health, ultimately leading to a more balanced and fulfilled life.

Chapter 2: Recognizing Your Emotions

Identifying Different Types of Emotions

Identifying different types of emotions is a fundamental aspect of emotional intelligence and self-care. Emotions can be categorized into basic types, such as happiness, sadness, anger, fear, surprise, and disgust. Each of these emotions serves a distinct purpose and can influence our thoughts and behaviors in significant ways. Understanding these basic emotions is the first step in recognizing how they manifest in our daily lives, allowing us to respond more effectively to our feelings and the situations that provoke them.

Happiness often arises from positive experiences, achievements, or meaningful relationships. It can be a fleeting feeling, but it is essential for our overall well-being. Recognizing moments of joy is crucial, as it encourages us to cultivate environments and activities that promote happiness. Journaling about these moments can reinforce positive experiences and help us understand what brings us fulfillment. On the other hand, sadness, while often viewed negatively, is a natural response to loss or disappointment. It can serve as a signal that something in our lives needs attention or change.

Anger is another common emotion that can be misunderstood. It often arises in response to perceived threats or injustices. While it can lead to destructive behaviors if not managed properly, anger also has the potential to motivate change and assert boundaries. Identifying the triggers of anger and employing techniques such as meditation can help in transforming this emotion into a constructive force rather than a harmful one. This practice requires self-awareness and a willingness to confront uncomfortable feelings rather than suppress them.

Fear is an emotion that can significantly impact our mental health. It often serves as a protective mechanism, alerting us to potential dangers. However, excessive fear can lead to anxiety and avoidance behaviors that hinder our daily functioning. Recognizing the sources of fear and understanding its role in our lives is crucial for effective self-care. Techniques such as mindfulness and deep breathing can help manage fear responses, allowing us to approach situations with a clearer mindset and greater emotional control.

Overall, emotions such as surprise and disgust play important roles in how we navigate our environments. Surprise can lead to heightened awareness and adaptability, while disgust can protect us from harmful experiences. By identifying and understanding these emotions, we empower ourselves to respond to life's challenges with resilience. Building a support system and knowing how to reach out when overwhelmed can further enhance our ability to manage emotions effectively. Accessing mental health resources also provides additional tools for emotional regulation, fostering a deeper understanding of our emotional landscapes.

The Connection Between Thoughts and Feelings

The connection between thoughts and feelings is a fundamental aspect of understanding mental health and emotional well-being. Our thoughts serve as the framework through which we interpret our experiences, influencing how we feel and react to various situations. Cognitive theories of psychology highlight that it is not the events themselves that cause our feelings, but rather the interpretations and beliefs we form about those events. For example, when faced with a challenging situation, a negative thought pattern may lead to feelings of anxiety or sadness, while a more constructive perspective could foster resilience and hope.

Engaging in self-care practices, such as journaling and meditation, provides valuable tools for exploring this connection. Journaling allows individuals to articulate their thoughts and emotions, creating a space for reflection and analysis. By examining their internal narratives, individuals can identify cognitive distortions that may exacerbate negative feelings. Meditation, on the other hand, encourages mindfulness, helping individuals observe their thoughts without immediate judgment or reaction. This practice can foster greater emotional regulation, allowing for a clearer distinction between thoughts and feelings, and ultimately leading to healthier coping mechanisms.

Emotional intelligence plays a crucial role in managing the relationship between thoughts and feelings. By developing the ability to recognize, understand, and manage one's own emotions, individuals can mitigate the impact of negative thought patterns. Understanding that feelings are often rooted in specific thoughts empowers individuals to challenge and reframe those thoughts. This process not only enhances self-awareness but also promotes empathy towards others, as it encourages a deeper understanding of how thoughts influence the emotional experiences of those around us.

Practicing self-compassion is essential in navigating the complexities of thoughts and feelings. When individuals encounter negative emotions, they often engage in harsh self-criticism, which can perpetuate a cycle of distress. By cultivating self-compassion, individuals learn to treat themselves with kindness and understanding, recognizing that experiencing difficult emotions is a universal aspect of the human experience. This shift in perspective can alleviate the burden of negative thoughts and foster a more balanced emotional state.

Knowing when and how to reach out for help is an integral part of managing thoughts and feelings effectively. A robust support system, whether comprised of friends, family, or mental health professionals, can provide essential guidance and perspective. Accessing mental health resources, such as counseling or support groups, enables individuals to share their experiences and gain insights on their emotional challenges. By fostering connections with others and utilizing available resources, individuals can navigate their thoughts and feelings more effectively, ultimately enhancing their overall mental health and emotional resilience.

Techniques for Emotional Awareness

Emotional awareness is a foundational aspect of mental health that allows individuals to understand and manage their feelings effectively. One of the most effective techniques for enhancing emotional awareness is meditation. This practice encourages individuals to observe their thoughts and feelings without judgment, fostering a deeper connection to their inner experiences. Mindfulness meditation, in particular, helps practitioners to stay present in the moment, which can reduce anxiety and increase emotional regulation. By dedicating just a few minutes each day to meditation, individuals can cultivate a greater awareness of their emotional states, leading to improved self-understanding and resilience.

Journaling is another powerful tool that can bolster emotional awareness. Writing about one's thoughts and feelings can provide clarity and insight into emotional patterns. When individuals take the time to reflect on their experiences, they can identify triggers for certain emotions and explore the underlying causes. This practice not only serves as an outlet for expression but also promotes self-reflection. Regular journaling can help individuals track their emotional progress, recognize recurring themes in their feelings, and ultimately develop a more nuanced understanding of their emotional landscape.

Time management plays a critical role in emotional awareness as well. When individuals effectively manage their time, they can create space for self-care activities that foster emotional intelligence. Allocating time for relaxation, hobbies, and social interactions can reduce stress and prevent feelings of overwhelm. Additionally, establishing a balanced schedule allows individuals to prioritize their mental health, making it easier to recognize when they are feeling stressed or emotionally drained. By being intentional about how they spend their time, individuals can cultivate an environment that supports emotional well-being.

Practicing self-compassion is essential for enhancing emotional awareness. This involves treating oneself with kindness and understanding during difficult times, rather than engaging in self-criticism. When individuals learn to be compassionate toward themselves, they are more likely to acknowledge their emotions without fear of judgment. This acceptance can lead to a more profound emotional awareness, as individuals become comfortable with their feelings and learn to respond to them constructively. Self-compassion also encourages individuals to seek help when needed, reinforcing the idea that reaching out for support is a sign of strength, not weakness.

Knowing when and how to reach out for help is a crucial aspect of emotional awareness. Understanding one's limits and recognizing when professional assistance is necessary can significantly impact mental health outcomes. Building a robust support system, whether through friends, family, or mental health resources, provides individuals with a safety net during challenging times. Accessing these resources can enhance emotional intelligence by providing different perspectives and coping strategies. By fostering connections with others and seeking appropriate support, individuals can navigate their emotional journeys more effectively, ultimately leading to improved mental health and well-being.

Chapter 3: The Science of Emotions

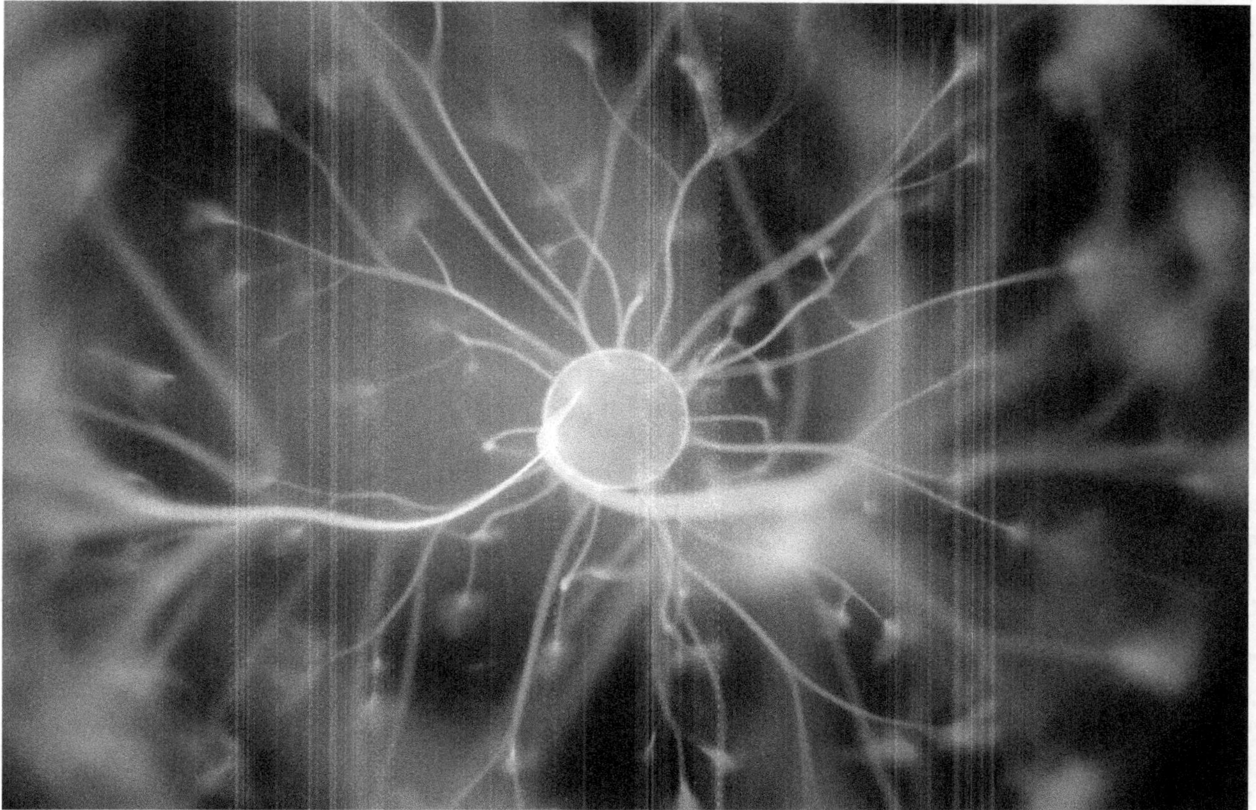

How Emotions Affect the Brain

Emotions play a pivotal role in shaping the functioning of the brain, influencing not only our thoughts but also our behaviors and overall mental health. When we experience emotions, whether they are positive or negative, specific neurological processes are activated. The limbic system, often referred to as the emotional center of the brain, processes these feelings and communicates with other brain regions, including the prefrontal cortex, which is responsible for decision-making and self-regulation. Understanding this connection is crucial for individuals seeking to enhance their emotional intelligence and practice effective self-care.

Positive emotions, such as joy and gratitude, can lead to the release of neurotransmitters like dopamine and serotonin, which promote feelings of well-being and happiness. These chemicals contribute to a state of mental balance and resilience, enabling individuals to approach challenges with a constructive mindset. On the other hand, negative emotions, such as stress and anxiety, can trigger the release of cortisol, a hormone that, when elevated over time, can lead to detrimental effects on both physical and mental health. Recognizing how these emotions affect brain chemistry can empower individuals to cultivate practices that promote emotional well-being.

The interplay between emotions and brain function underscores the importance of emotional regulation. Techniques such as meditation and journaling can be particularly effective in managing emotional responses. Meditation, for instance, has been shown to alter brain structures associated with emotional regulation, enhancing an individual's ability to control their reactions to stressors. Journaling, on the other hand, provides an outlet for processing emotions, allowing individuals to reflect on their feelings and gain clarity. By integrating these practices into daily routines, individuals can foster a healthier emotional landscape.

Self-compassion is another vital component in the way emotions affect the brain. Research indicates that cultivating a sense of self-kindness can buffer against negative emotional states and promote a greater sense of well-being. When individuals practice self-compassion, they activate brain regions associated with emotional regulation and social connection, which can lead to improved resilience in the face of adversity. This understanding highlights the significance of being gentle with oneself during difficult times, emphasizing that self-care is not just an act but a crucial aspect of emotional health.

Understanding when and how to ask for help is absolutely essential for emotional well-being and overall mental health. Acknowledging that emotions can significantly affect brain function serves as a powerful motivator for individuals to seek support when necessary. Whether it is through professional mental health services, such as therapy or counseling, or through caring social connections with friends and family, obtaining help can be a crucial step in aiding emotional processing and promoting healing. By actively developing emotional intelligence and becoming more aware of how emotions influence brain function and behavior, people can manage their mental health journeys more effectively. This awareness not only enhances their ability to cope with challenges but also improves their overall quality of life, resilience, and capacity to thrive in various aspects of life.

The Physiological Responses to Emotions

Emotions are not merely abstract experiences; they trigger a complex array of physiological responses within our bodies. When we encounter situations that elicit strong feelings, such as joy, anger, fear, or sadness, our body reacts in specific ways. This response is primarily governed by the autonomic nervous system, which consists of the sympathetic and parasympathetic divisions. The sympathetic nervous system prepares the body for a 'fight or flight' response, increasing heart rate, blood pressure, and breathing rate, while the parasympathetic system promotes a 'rest and digest' state, facilitating recovery and relaxation. Understanding these physiological reactions can enhance our emotional intelligence and self-awareness, essential components of effective self-care.

The connection between emotional experiences and physiological responses highlights the importance of recognizing these signals in our bodies. For instance, anxiety might manifest as a racing heart or shallow breathing, while sadness could lead to fatigue and muscle tension. By learning to identify these physical cues, individuals can develop a more nuanced understanding of their emotional states. This awareness is a critical step in managing emotions effectively, as it allows for timely interventions, such as practicing mindfulness or engaging in deep-breathing exercises. These techniques not only help regulate physiological responses but also foster a greater sense of control over one's emotions.

Incorporating practices like meditation and journaling into daily routines can significantly influence how we respond to emotional stimuli. Meditation encourages a state of mindfulness, which helps in observing emotions without immediate reaction. This practice can lead to changes in brain activity, reducing stress and enhancing emotional regulation. Similarly, journaling provides an outlet for processing emotions, allowing individuals to articulate their feelings and reflect on their physiological responses. By documenting emotional experiences, one may identify patterns and triggers, paving the way for more effective self-care strategies.

Self-compassion plays a vital role in how we respond to our emotions and physiological reactions. When individuals adopt a compassionate stance towards themselves, they are more likely to engage in healthy coping mechanisms rather than resorting to harmful behaviors. This compassionate approach can mitigate the negative physiological effects of stress and emotional turmoil, promoting overall well-being. By fostering a supportive internal dialogue, individuals can navigate their emotional landscapes more effectively, nurturing resilience and a positive self-image.

Recognizing when to reach out for help is essential in managing emotional and physiological responses. Building a robust support system can provide the necessary resources and encouragement to cope with challenging emotions. Whether through professional mental health services, support groups, or trusted friends and family, having access to external support can significantly enhance one's ability to process emotions healthily. It is crucial to remember that seeking help is a sign of strength, not weakness. By integrating self-care practices and acknowledging the physiological impacts of emotions, individuals can cultivate a more balanced and resilient mental health landscape.

The Impact of Emotions on Behavior

Emotions play a crucial role in shaping our behaviors and decision-making processes. Understanding the impact of emotions on our actions is essential for developing emotional intelligence and enhancing self-care practices. Emotions can drive us towards positive behaviors, such as seeking support, practicing self-compassion, or engaging in healthy coping mechanisms like meditation and journaling. Conversely, unregulated emotions can lead to impulsive decisions, avoidance behaviors, or unhealthy coping strategies, further exacerbating stress and mental health challenges.

When we experience intense emotions, they often trigger physiological responses that influence our behavior. For instance, feelings of anxiety can lead to avoidance of certain situations, while anger may result in confrontational behaviors. Recognizing these emotional triggers is a fundamental aspect of emotional intelligence, as it allows individuals to pause and reflect before reacting. By developing an awareness of how emotions influence our choices, we can implement strategies to regulate our feelings, leading to more constructive outcomes in our daily lives.

Self-care practices such as meditation and journaling serve as effective tools for managing emotions and, consequently, behaviors. Meditation encourages mindfulness, helping individuals to observe their thoughts and feelings without judgment. This practice fosters a deeper understanding of emotional responses and creates space for healthier reactions. Journaling, on the other hand, provides an outlet for expressing and processing emotions, allowing individuals to identify patterns in their behavior linked to specific feelings. By engaging in these techniques, individuals can cultivate a greater sense of emotional control and resilience.

Building a support system is another crucial aspect of managing the interplay between emotions and behavior. When we encounter challenging emotions, having a network of supportive friends, family, or mental health professionals can provide essential guidance and encouragement. Knowing when and how to reach out for help is a vital skill in self-care, as it can prevent negative behaviors stemming from emotional distress. Open communication within a support system fosters an environment where emotions can be shared and understood, ultimately leading to healthier coping mechanisms.

Accessing mental health resources is key to navigating the complexities of emotions and behaviors. Educational programs, workshops, and therapeutic resources can equip individuals with the knowledge and skills necessary to enhance their emotional intelligence. These resources often promote self-care techniques and provide strategies for recognizing and controlling emotions effectively. By prioritizing emotional well-being and understanding its impact on behavior, individuals can create a balanced and fulfilling life rooted in self-awareness and compassion.

Chapter 4: Regulating Your Emotions

Strategies for Emotional Regulation

Emotional regulation is a crucial skill that can significantly enhance mental health and well-being. It involves the ability to recognize, understand, and manage one's emotions in a constructive manner. One effective strategy for emotional regulation is mindfulness meditation. This practice encourages individuals to focus on the present moment, acknowledging their thoughts and feelings without judgment. By regularly engaging in mindfulness meditation, one can develop greater awareness of emotional triggers and patterns, allowing for more thoughtful responses rather than impulsive reactions. This increased awareness not only fosters emotional intelligence but also cultivates a sense of inner peace and resilience in the face of stress.

Journaling is another powerful tool for emotional regulation. Writing about one's thoughts and feelings provides an outlet for expression and reflection. It can help clarify emotions, identify patterns, and explore underlying issues contributing to stress or anxiety. Regularly engaging in journaling encourages individuals to process their experiences, leading to greater self-understanding and emotional clarity. Additionally, the act of writing can serve as a cathartic release, allowing individuals to cope with overwhelming emotions and gain perspective on challenging situations. By incorporating journaling into a self-care routine, individuals can enhance their emotional well-being and develop healthier coping mechanisms.

Time management plays a significant role in emotional regulation as well. A well-structured schedule can reduce feelings of overwhelm and anxiety by providing a clear framework for daily activities. Prioritizing tasks and setting realistic deadlines can help create a sense of control over one's environment, which is essential for emotional stability. Implementing techniques such as the Pomodoro Technique or time-blocking can promote focus and efficiency, allowing individuals to allocate time for self-care and relaxation. Balancing responsibilities with leisure activities is vital, as it fosters a sense of fulfillment and prevents burnout. By mastering time management skills, individuals can minimize stress and create space for emotional balance.

Practicing self-compassion is an essential strategy for emotional regulation. It involves treating oneself with kindness and understanding, especially during difficult times. Self-compassion allows individuals to acknowledge their struggles without harsh self-criticism, fostering a more nurturing inner dialogue. This approach can mitigate feelings of shame and inadequacy, which often exacerbate emotional distress. Engaging in positive affirmations and reminding oneself that it is okay to experience difficult emotions can enhance resilience. By cultivating self-compassion, individuals can better navigate the ups and downs of life while maintaining a healthier emotional state.

Knowing when and how to seek help is essential for managing emotions. Creating a strong support network—comprising friends, family, or mental health professionals—can be invaluable during challenging times. Understanding that requesting help is a sign of strength rather than a weakness can encourage people to focus on their emotional health. Engaging with mental health resources such as therapy or support groups can offer additional strategies for handling emotions effectively. By fostering connections and asking for help when needed, individuals can enhance their emotional regulation skills and cultivate a more resilient mindset.

Mindfulness and Its Role in Emotion Regulation

Mindfulness is a powerful practice that involves paying deliberate attention to the present moment without judgment. In the context of emotion regulation, mindfulness serves as a foundational tool that allows individuals to observe their thoughts and feelings without becoming overwhelmed by them. This heightened awareness fosters a deeper understanding of one's emotional responses, enabling a person to identify triggers and patterns. By cultivating mindfulness, individuals can create a mental space that facilitates more thoughtful reactions to emotional experiences rather than impulsive responses that may lead to further distress.

The practice of mindfulness can be integrated into various self-care techniques, such as meditation and journaling. Through meditation, individuals learn to focus on their breath or specific sensations in the body, which helps ground them in the present moment. This practice not only reduces stress but also enhances emotional clarity. Journaling complements this by providing a reflective outlet for exploring thoughts and feelings. Writing about emotional experiences allows individuals to process their feelings and recognize recurring themes, ultimately leading to improved emotional regulation and self-awareness.

Furthermore, mindfulness enhances emotional intelligence by encouraging individuals to acknowledge and validate their emotions. Rather than suppressing or ignoring feelings, mindfulness promotes acceptance, which is crucial for effective emotion regulation. By understanding that all emotions are valid, individuals can approach their emotional landscape with compassion and curiosity. This acceptance can lead to healthier coping mechanisms, as individuals become more adept at distinguishing between emotions and responding appropriately to them, rather than reacting out of fear or anxiety.

Mindfulness also plays a significant role in developing self-compassion, which is essential for emotional well-being. As individuals practice being present with their emotions, they learn to treat themselves with kindness during difficult times. This shift in perspective can reduce feelings of shame or inadequacy, which often accompany negative emotions. Self-compassion encourages individuals to respond to their emotional challenges with understanding and care, fostering a more supportive inner dialogue that promotes resilience and emotional stability.

Incorporating mindfulness into daily life can enhance an individual's ability to seek support when needed. By being in tune with their emotions, individuals can better recognize when they may require help from friends, family, or mental health professionals. Mindfulness encourages open communication about emotional needs, making it easier to reach out and access resources. This proactive approach not only strengthens personal support systems but also reinforces the importance of community in mental health management, ultimately leading to a more balanced and fulfilling life.

Journaling as a Tool for Emotional Clarity

Journaling serves as a powerful tool for achieving emotional clarity, offering individuals a structured space to articulate their thoughts and feelings. In our fast-paced, modern world, where emotions can often become overwhelming, the act of writing can facilitate a deeper understanding of one's internal landscape. By putting pen to paper, individuals can explore their emotions, identify patterns, and reflect on the experiences that shape their mental health. This practice encourages mindfulness, allowing for a moment of pause in which one can examine their thoughts without judgment, ultimately promoting emotional awareness and clarity.

The benefits of journaling extend beyond mere expression; it also aids in processing complex emotions. When individuals confront difficult feelings—such as anxiety, sadness, or anger—journaling provides a non-threatening outlet to explore these sensations. Writing about a distressing event or feeling can help untangle the emotions associated with it, making it easier to understand and manage. This practice not only fosters emotional intelligence but also reinforces the notion that it is okay to experience a wide range of feelings, thereby encouraging self-compassion and acceptance.

Incorporating journaling into a self-care routine can also enhance stress management techniques. Regularly dedicating time to write can serve as a release valve for pent-up emotions, alleviating stress and promoting mental well-being. This practice can be particularly useful during challenging times, as it provides clarity and perspective that may be hard to attain in moments of turmoil. By documenting daily stressors and responses, individuals can identify triggers and develop healthier coping strategies, leading to improved emotional regulation and resilience.

Journaling can foster a greater sense of connection to oneself, acting as a mirror that reflects both strengths and areas for growth. Through this reflective practice, individuals can track their emotional journeys, recognizing progress over time and celebrating achievements, no matter how small. This self-awareness not only enhances emotional intelligence but also encourages individuals to reach out for support when necessary. Understanding one's emotional state can facilitate more open conversations with friends, family, or mental health professionals, creating a supportive network that is crucial for mental health.

Journaling is more than just a solitary activity; it can be a bridge to broader mental health resources. By documenting their feelings and experiences, individuals may become more attuned to when they need additional support. It can serve as a catalyst for seeking help or finding community resources that align with their emotional needs. In this way, journaling becomes a vital component of a holistic approach to self-care, empowering individuals to take charge of their mental health while fostering a deeper connection with themselves and their support systems.

Chapter 5: Self-Compassion and Emotional Intelligence

Understanding Self-Compassion

Self-compassion is an essential component of mental well-being that involves treating oneself with kindness, understanding, and support during difficult times. Recognizing our shared human experience is crucial; everyone faces challenges, makes mistakes, and experiences feelings of inadequacy. Instead of succumbing to self-criticism or isolation, self-compassion encourages individuals to acknowledge their struggles and respond to them with warmth and care, similar to how one would treat a friend in distress. This gentle approach fosters resilience and emotional stability, making it a vital practice for enhancing mental health.

At the heart of self-compassion are three core elements: self-kindness, common humanity, and mindfulness. Self-kindness refers to being warm and understanding towards ourselves when we suffer, fail, or feel inadequate, rather than harshly critiquing ourselves. Common humanity emphasizes the recognition that suffering and personal inadequacy are part of the shared human experience, which helps combat feelings of isolation and loneliness. Mindfulness involves maintaining a balanced awareness of negative emotions, acknowledging them without over-identifying or suppressing them. Together, these elements create a foundation for a healthier self-relationship and psychological resilience.

Practicing self-compassion can significantly impact emotional intelligence, as it encourages individuals to recognize and accept their feelings without judgment. This acceptance fosters greater emotional awareness, allowing for a deeper understanding of one's responses to stress and adversity. By developing self-compassion, individuals can cultivate a more profound emotional intelligence that enhances their ability to empathize with others, manage their emotions effectively, and navigate interpersonal relationships. This growth not only benefits the individual but also contributes to a more supportive and understanding community.

Incorporating self-compassion into daily life can be achieved through various techniques, such as journaling, meditation, and affirmations. Journaling provides a safe space for reflection, allowing individuals to explore their thoughts and emotions while practicing self-kindness. Mindfulness meditation encourages present-moment awareness and acceptance, which can help alleviate negative self-talk and foster compassion. Additionally, positive affirmations can reinforce self-worth and encourage a nurturing inner dialogue. These techniques serve as practical tools for individuals seeking to enhance their self-compassion and overall mental health.

Understanding and practicing self-compassion is a transformative journey that equips individuals with the tools necessary for emotional resilience and well-being. By embracing self-kindness, recognizing our shared humanity, and cultivating mindfulness, we pave the way for healthier relationships with ourselves and others. As we prioritize self-care and mental health awareness, incorporating self-compassion into our lives can lead to profound changes in how we navigate challenges, manage stress, and seek support when needed.

The Link Between Self-Compassion and Emotional Resilience

Self-compassion is a vital component of emotional resilience, serving as a protective factor against the challenges of modern life. When individuals practice self-compassion, they cultivate a nurturing internal dialogue that allows them to acknowledge their imperfections and failures without harsh self-judgment. This acceptance can lead to a more balanced emotional state, as it fosters a sense of understanding and kindness towards oneself during tough times. As a result, self-compassion not only alleviates feelings of inadequacy but also strengthens an individual's ability to cope with stress and adversity.

Research has consistently shown that self-compassion is closely linked to various aspects of emotional intelligence. Those who engage in self-compassionate practices are more likely to develop greater emotional awareness and regulation. By recognizing their emotional states and responding to them with care, individuals can navigate through difficult feelings more effectively. This emotional intelligence enables them to manage stressors with a level of grace and resilience that those lacking self-compassion may struggle to achieve. As they learn to respond to their emotional experiences with empathy, they enhance their ability to withstand life's inevitable challenges.

Self-compassion encourages the development of a supportive inner voice, which can counteract negative thoughts and beliefs. This internal support system is essential for building emotional resilience, as it fosters a sense of belonging and connection, even in moments of solitude. Individuals who practice self-compassion are less likely to isolate themselves during hard times; instead, they recognize that struggle is a shared human experience. This understanding can motivate them to reach out for help when needed, reinforcing their support networks and enhancing their overall emotional well-being.

Incorporating self-compassion into daily routines, through techniques such as meditation and journaling, can significantly bolster emotional resilience. Mindfulness practices help individuals to observe their thoughts and feelings without judgment, promoting a compassionate stance towards themselves. Journaling provides an avenue for reflection and self-expression, allowing individuals to articulate their struggles while nurturing self-kindness. By engaging in these practices regularly, people can develop a resilient mindset that empowers them to face challenges with confidence and grace.

The link between self-compassion and emotional resilience underscores the importance of prioritizing mental health and self-care in our modern lives. By fostering a compassionate relationship with oneself, individuals lay the groundwork for effectively managing stress, enhancing emotional intelligence, and building supportive connections. As they learn to embrace their vulnerabilities and imperfections, they cultivate a resilience that not only benefits themselves but also encourages a culture of empathy and understanding within their communities.

Practices to Cultivate Self-Compassion

Practicing self-compassion is essential for fostering emotional resilience and promoting overall mental well-being. Self-compassion involves treating oneself with kindness, recognizing one's shared humanity, and embracing the inevitability of imperfection. By cultivating self-compassion, individuals can create a healthier relationship with themselves, which is vital for effective self-care. To begin this journey, it is important to develop a mindful awareness of one's thoughts and feelings. This means observing internal experiences without judgment and acknowledging emotions as valid responses to life's challenges.

One effective technique for nurturing self-compassion is through meditation. Mindfulness meditation encourages individuals to focus on the present moment and cultivate a sense of acceptance towards their thoughts and feelings. Guided meditations specifically designed for self-compassion can help foster a nurturing inner voice. By regularly practicing these meditations, individuals can gradually shift their mindset from self-criticism to self-kindness, allowing for greater emotional balance and resilience in the face of stress.

Writing is another powerful practice that can enhance self-compassion. Writing about personal experiences, feelings, and challenges can provide clarity and perspective. Individuals can reflect on their mistakes and hardships while consciously framing their narratives in a compassionate light. For instance, instead of harshly criticizing oneself for a perceived failure, one may explore what can be learned from the experience and how it contributes to personal growth. This practice not only helps in processing emotions but also reinforces the understanding that everyone faces difficulties and setbacks.

Time management plays a crucial role in self-compassion. By prioritizing self-care and allocating time for relaxation and reflection, individuals can prevent burnout and emotional exhaustion. Creating a balanced schedule that includes time for activities that bring joy, fulfillment, and rest can promote a healthier mindset. It is important to remember that taking time for oneself is not selfish but rather an essential component of maintaining mental health. This balance allows for a greater capacity to show compassion toward oneself and others.

Once again, recognizing when to reach out for help is a vital aspect of self-compassion. Acknowledging that one cannot navigate life's challenges alone is not a sign of weakness but a demonstration of strength. Building a support system, whether through friends, family, or mental health professionals, can provide the necessary encouragement and understanding. Accessing resources such as therapy or support groups can further enhance self-compassion, as these avenues offer validation and guidance in overcoming struggles. By fostering a compassionate approach to oneself and seeking help when needed, individuals can create a robust foundation for mental health and emotional well-being.

Chapter 6: Stress Management Techniques

Identifying Sources of Stress

Identifying sources of stress is a crucial first step in managing mental health effectively. Stress can arise from various aspects of life, including work, relationships, financial pressures, and personal expectations. Understanding where stress originates allows individuals to implement targeted self-care strategies. For instance, keeping a stress diary can help identify patterns and specific triggers that lead to heightened stress levels. This awareness not only fosters emotional intelligence but also empowers individuals to make informed decisions regarding their mental well-being.

One common source of stress is the pressure to meet external expectations, whether from employers, family members, or societal norms. This pressure can lead to feelings of inadequacy and anxiety, particularly when individuals believe they are falling short. Recognizing the influence of these external factors can help individuals develop a more compassionate relationship with themselves, allowing them to prioritize their mental health over unrealistic standards. Embracing self-compassion involves understanding that it is normal to struggle and that seeking balance is a healthy pursuit.

Another significant source of stress is the internal dialogue that often accompanies self-criticism. Individuals may engage in negative self-talk that exacerbates feelings of worthlessness or failure. By practicing mindfulness and emotional regulation techniques, individuals can learn to recognize these harmful thought patterns and reframe them into more constructive narratives. Journaling can also serve as a valuable tool for this process, as it provides a safe space to explore emotions and challenge negative beliefs.

Time management is another essential aspect of stress identification. Poor time management can lead to overwhelming workloads and unmet deadlines, contributing to chronic stress. By evaluating how time is spent and prioritizing tasks, individuals can create a more balanced schedule that allows for breaks and self-care practices. This proactive approach not only mitigates stress but also enhances productivity and overall well-being.

Social relationships can be both a source of stress and a potential support system. Identifying toxic or unfulfilling relationships is essential for mental health. Understanding when to set boundaries or seek new connections can significantly improve emotional resilience. Knowing when and how to reach out for help is crucial; whether through friends, family, or professional resources, building a robust support network can provide relief and guidance in navigating stress. Accessing mental health resources, such as therapy or support groups, can further empower individuals to manage their stress effectively and cultivate a healthier mindset.

Stress Reduction Techniques

Stress can significantly impact mental health, highlighting the importance of effective stress reduction techniques. One of the most widely practiced methods is meditation, which promotes mindfulness and relaxation. Regular meditation helps individuals gain better control over their thoughts, enabling them to focus on the present moment rather than becoming overwhelmed by past regrets or future anxieties. Various forms of meditation, such as guided sessions, mantra meditation, or even mindfulness walks, can be tailored to individual preferences, making it an accessible tool for anyone seeking to improve their mental well-being.

Journaling serves as another powerful technique for managing stress. By writing down thoughts and feelings, individuals can gain clarity and insight into their emotional states. This practice not only aids in processing experiences but also helps in identifying stress triggers. Regularly reflecting on one's emotions through journaling fosters emotional intelligence, allowing individuals to recognize patterns in their behavior and responses. This self-awareness is crucial for developing coping strategies and cultivating resilience in the face of stress.

In addition to journaling, simply writing a list of the issues that were bothering you can effectively help you identify your triggers and things you should try to avoid in the future. Additionally, don't forget to create a list of the things that also brought you happiness and joy. This can be similar to weighing pros and cons, allowing you to gain a clearer understanding of what positively influences your well-being.

Effective time management plays a vital role in stress reduction as well. Often, stress arises from feeling overwhelmed by responsibilities and deadlines. By prioritizing tasks and breaking them into manageable steps, individuals can create a structured approach to their daily lives. Tools such as planners or digital apps can assist in scheduling time effectively, ensuring that there is room for both obligations and personal self-care activities. This balance is essential for maintaining mental health, as it allows individuals to dedicate time to relaxation and rejuvenation.

Practicing self-compassion is equally important in managing stress. Individuals often hold themselves to high standards, leading to feelings of inadequacy when they fall short. By cultivating an attitude of kindness towards oneself, it becomes easier to navigate challenges without excessive self-criticism. Self-compassion encourages a supportive internal dialogue, which can buffer against the negative effects of stress. This approach not only enhances emotional resilience but also promotes a healthier relationship with oneself, fostering a more positive mindset.

Knowing when and how to reach out for help is crucial for effective stress management. Building a support system of friends, family, or mental health professionals can provide essential resources during challenging times. Engaging in open conversations about mental health and stress can help reduce stigma and promote understanding. Accessing mental health resources, such as therapy or community support groups, can further empower individuals to manage stress more effectively. Recognizing the importance of support and connection enhances one's ability to cope with stressors, ultimately contributing to a healthier mental state.

The Role of Emotional Intelligence in Stress Management

Emotional intelligence (EI) plays a crucial role in stress management, acting as a buffer against the various pressures and challenges individuals face in their daily lives. Defined as the ability to recognize, understand, and manage our own emotions while also being aware of and influencing the emotions of others, emotional intelligence encompasses several key components, including self-awareness, self-regulation, motivation, empathy, and social skills. By cultivating these aspects of emotional intelligence, individuals can better navigate stressors, maintain a healthy mindset, and enhance their overall well-being.

Self-awareness is the cornerstone of emotional intelligence and serves as the first step in effective stress management. When individuals are aware of their emotional triggers and responses, they can identify when stress levels are rising and take proactive measures to mitigate its impact. This might involve employing techniques like journaling to reflect on feelings or practicing mindfulness meditation to ground oneself in the present moment. Recognizing emotions allows individuals to differentiate between constructive and destructive responses to stress, enabling them to choose healthier coping strategies.

Self-regulation, another vital element of emotional intelligence, equips individuals with the tools to manage their emotional responses to stressors. By developing self-control and resilience, individuals can prevent their emotions from overriding rational thinking. This is particularly important when faced with high-pressure situations, as it helps to maintain composure and clarity. Techniques such as deep-breathing exercises, progressive muscle relaxation, or guided imagery can support self-regulation, allowing individuals to respond thoughtfully rather than react impulsively when confronted with stress.

Empathy and social skills, also integral to emotional intelligence, facilitate the formation of supportive relationships that are essential for effective stress management. Understanding the emotions of others fosters connections that can provide emotional support during challenging times. Building a robust support system enables individuals to share their experiences and seek help when needed, reducing feelings of isolation. Engaging in open communication and practicing active listening within relationships can cultivate a sense of belonging and mutual understanding, which is vital for emotional resilience.

Incorporating emotional intelligence into daily life not only enhances personal well-being but also contributes to healthier interactions with others. As individuals learn to recognize and manage their emotions, they become more adept at identifying the emotional needs of those around them. This reciprocal understanding can lead to stronger, more supportive communities, ultimately creating an environment where mental health awareness is prioritized. By actively practicing self-compassion and understanding when to reach out for help, individuals position themselves to harness the full potential of emotional intelligence in managing stress and promoting overall mental health.

Chapter 7: Building a Support System

The Importance of Social Support

Social support plays a crucial role in maintaining mental health and well-being. It encompasses the emotional, informational, and practical assistance provided by friends, family, and community members. In today's fast-paced and often isolating world, recognizing the importance of social support is vital for individuals seeking to enhance their self-care practices. A strong support system can act as a buffer against stress and adversity, helping individuals navigate life's challenges with greater resilience. By fostering connections, individuals not only enhance their emotional intelligence but also cultivate a sense of belonging that is essential for mental well-being.

Research consistently shows that individuals with robust social support networks experience lower levels of anxiety and depression. Engaging with others allows for the sharing of experiences, which can provide validation and understanding. This exchange can be particularly beneficial when practicing techniques like meditation and journaling. For instance, sharing insights or challenges faced during meditation can lead to deeper self-understanding and growth. Moreover, discussing journaling experiences can inspire new perspectives, enriching one's self-care journey. This mutual support encourages individuals to express their emotions, facilitating greater emotional awareness and control.

Social support is instrumental in stress management. In times of high stress, the presence of a supportive network can significantly influence how individuals cope with challenges. Supportive relationships provide a safe space to express feelings without judgment, fostering an environment where individuals can practice self-compassion. This environment encourages open dialogue about mental health struggles, which is essential for recognizing when professional help may be needed. Understanding that reaching out for help is a sign of strength, rather than weakness, can empower individuals to seek out mental health resources when necessary.

Building a strong support system requires intentional effort and communication. Individuals are encouraged to identify potential sources of support within their networks, whether they be family members, friends, coworkers, or online communities focused on mental health. By nurturing these relationships, individuals can create a web of support that enhances their emotional intelligence and overall well-being. Engaging in activities that promote connection, such as group meditation sessions or journaling workshops, can further strengthen these bonds, providing both social interaction and shared growth opportunities.

Accessing mental health resources is an integral part of a comprehensive self-care strategy. Many individuals may feel uncertain about where to start, but utilizing social support can lead to valuable recommendations and guidance. Friends or family members who have sought mental health assistance can offer insights into local therapists, support groups, or online platforms. By leveraging these resources, individuals can take informed steps towards improving their mental health. In conclusion, prioritizing social support not only enhances self-care practices but also cultivates a resilient mindset, enabling individuals to thrive in their mental health journeys.

How to Cultivate Meaningful Relationships

Cultivating meaningful relationships is a cornerstone of mental health and self-care. Meaningful connections not only provide emotional support but also enhance overall well-being. To foster these relationships, it is essential to begin with self-awareness. Understanding your own emotions, triggers, and needs allows you to communicate more effectively with others. Engaging in practices such as journaling can help clarify your thoughts and feelings, making it easier to express them in your interactions. This self-reflection forms the foundation for building deeper connections with those around you.

Emotional intelligence plays a vital role in nurturing relationships. Being attuned to your own emotions and the emotions of others enhances empathy and strengthens bonds. To develop this skill, practice active listening by fully engaging in conversations without distractions. Acknowledge others' feelings and validate their experiences, which fosters trust and openness. When people feel heard and understood, they are more likely to reciprocate, creating a cycle of support and connection that benefits all parties involved.

Another critical aspect of cultivating meaningful relationships is setting healthy boundaries. Recognizing your limits and communicating them clearly helps maintain a balanced dynamic. Boundaries protect your mental health and provide a framework for mutual respect. It is important to be assertive about your needs while remaining open to compromise. This approach not only strengthens relationships but also demonstrates self-compassion, as you prioritize your well-being alongside the needs of others.

Reaching out for help is often necessary in the journey of self-care and relationship building. It is essential to identify when you need support and to know how to seek it. Establishing a reliable support system, whether through friends, family, or mental health professionals, can alleviate feelings of isolation. Sharing your struggles with trusted individuals fosters deeper connections and facilitates healing. Remember that vulnerability is a strength; it encourages others to open up and share their own experiences, enriching your relationships further.

Accessing mental health resources can enhance your ability to cultivate and maintain meaningful relationships. Workshops, therapy, or support groups provide valuable tools and techniques for improving communication, managing stress, and developing emotional resilience. Investing time in these resources not only benefits your personal growth but also equips you with the skills necessary to nurture the relationships that are vital to your mental health. By prioritizing self-care and fostering meaningful connections, you create a supportive network that enhances both your life and the lives of those around you.

Reaching Out for Help: When and How

Recognizing when to reach out for help is a crucial aspect of maintaining mental health. Many individuals struggle with the stigma associated with seeking assistance, often believing that they should handle their problems independently. However, acknowledging the need for support is a sign of strength, not weakness. It's essential to understand that everyone faces challenges, and reaching out can be a vital step toward recovery and well-being. Signs that you may need help include persistent feelings of sadness, anxiety, or anger that interfere with daily activities, difficulty managing stress, or feelings of isolation. Understanding these signs is the first step in fostering emotional intelligence and self-awareness.

Once the decision to seek help is made, the next step is determining how to do so effectively. There are various avenues available, including speaking with friends, family members, or mental health professionals. It can be helpful to start by discussing your feelings with someone you trust, as this can provide immediate emotional support and validation. If the issues persist or if you seek more structured guidance, consider reaching out to a therapist or counselor. They can offer professional insights and coping strategies tailored to your unique situation. It is important to remember that seeking help is not a one-time event but an ongoing process that may require multiple approaches.

When reaching out for help, it's beneficial to prepare for the conversation. Articulate your feelings and experiences as clearly as possible, as this can facilitate better understanding and communication. Journaling can be a useful tool in this preparation phase, allowing you to process your thoughts and emotions before discussing them with someone else. Additionally, practicing self-compassion during this time can alleviate feelings of guilt or shame about needing help. Remind yourself that everyone encounters challenges, and seeking assistance is a healthy and proactive choice.

Establishing a support system is another critical component of mental health management. Surrounding yourself with individuals who are empathetic and understanding can significantly enhance your ability to cope with stress and emotional turmoil. This support can come from various sources, including friends, family, support groups, or online communities. Engaging with others who share similar experiences can foster a sense of belonging and reduce feelings of isolation. It is essential to nurture these relationships and express your needs, as effective communication within your support system can lead to more meaningful connections and support.

Accessing mental health resources is an integral part of the help-seeking process. Numerous organizations offer hotlines, online resources, and local services designed to assist those in need. Familiarizing yourself with these options can empower you to take action when necessary. In addition to professional help, consider integrating self-care techniques such as meditation and time management into your routine. These practices can enhance your emotional resilience and improve your overall mental health. Remember that reaching out for help is a courageous step toward healing and that you are not alone on this journey.

Chapter 8: Accessing Mental Health Resources

Understanding Available Mental Health Resources

Understanding available mental health resources is essential for anyone on a journey of self-care and emotional well-being. In today's fast-paced world, mental health challenges are increasingly common, and it's crucial to recognize that help is available. Resources can take various forms, including professional therapy, community support groups, online platforms, and self-help materials. Familiarizing oneself with these options not only empowers individuals to seek assistance when needed but also enhances their overall understanding of mental health.

Professional therapy is one of the most recognized forms of mental health support. Psychologists, counselors, and therapists offer a safe space for individuals to explore their thoughts and feelings. These professionals are trained to provide evidence-based techniques tailored to an individual's unique situation. Therapy can address a range of issues from anxiety and depression to relationship difficulties and stress management. Understanding the types of therapy available, such as cognitive-behavioral therapy or mindfulness-based approaches, can help individuals choose the right path for their needs.

In addition to professional help, community support groups play a vital role in mental health resources. These groups often provide a sense of belonging and shared experience, which can be incredibly healing. Participants can connect with others who face similar challenges, allowing for mutual support and understanding. Many organizations host regular meetings, both in-person and online, focused on specific issues such as grief, addiction, or chronic illness. Engaging in these communities fosters emotional intelligence as individuals learn to recognize and articulate their feelings in a supportive environment.

The digital age has brought forth a wealth of online mental health resources that cater to diverse needs. Mobile applications and websites offer tools for meditation, journaling, and stress management that are easily accessible. Many platforms provide guided mindfulness exercises, mood tracking, and educational resources that encourage self-reflection and personal growth. These resources can be particularly beneficial for those who may feel intimidated by traditional therapy settings or for those seeking supplementary tools to enhance their self-care practices. Learning how to effectively utilize these digital resources can significantly improve one's mental health management.

Knowing when and how to reach out for help is a critical component of understanding mental health resources. It is essential to recognize the signs of emotional distress, such as persistent sadness, overwhelming anxiety, or difficulty functioning in daily life. Acknowledging these feelings and understanding that seeking help is a sign of strength is vital. Encouragingly, many resources are designed to be approachable and user-friendly, making it easier for individuals to take that first step. Building a support system that includes friends, family, and mental health professionals can create a safety net, ensuring that help is always within reach when needed.

How to Navigate Mental Health Services

Navigating mental health services can feel overwhelming, especially for individuals who are just beginning to prioritize their mental well-being. Understanding the landscape of mental health services is crucial for effectively accessing the support you need. Start by familiarizing yourself with the different types of mental health professionals available, including psychologists, psychiatrists, social workers, and counselors. Each professional has unique training and areas of expertise, which means they offer different types of services. Researching their qualifications and identifying which professional aligns with your needs is an essential first step.

Once you have a sense of who you might want to consult, consider how to initiate contact. Many mental health services offer initial consultations, which can provide insight into what to expect from therapy or treatment. It's important to approach this first step with an open mind. Prepare a list of questions to ask during your consultation, such as the therapist's approach to treatment, their experience with specific concerns, and how they measure progress. This not only helps you gauge their suitability but also empowers you to take an active role in your mental health journey.

After selecting a professional, setting realistic expectations for your sessions is vital. Mental health treatment is often a gradual process, requiring patience and commitment. It's helpful to establish a routine that includes regular appointments, as consistency can lead to better outcomes. Additionally, consider integrating self-care practices such as meditation, journaling, or emotional intelligence exercises into your daily life. These practices can complement your therapy sessions and enhance your overall mental wellness.

Recognizing when you need help is another crucial aspect of navigating mental health services. Self-awareness plays a significant role in determining when to seek assistance. If you find that self-care techniques are no longer effective or that your emotional state is impacting your daily life, it may be time to reach out for professional support. Don't hesitate to discuss your feelings with trusted friends or family members; they can often provide insight and encouragement to take that next step.

Finding a support system is instrumental in your mental health journey. This can include friends, family, support groups, or online communities focused on mental health awareness. Engaging with others who share similar experiences can foster a sense of belonging and reduce feelings of isolation. Remember that seeking help is a sign of strength, and building a network of support can enhance your resilience as you navigate the complexities of mental health services.

The Role of Professional Help in Emotional Intelligence

The journey toward enhancing emotional intelligence often intersects with the need for professional help. While self-care practices such as meditation, journaling, and effective time management can significantly contribute to personal growth, there are instances where the complexities of emotional challenges require expert guidance. Mental health professionals, including therapists and counselors, possess the training and experience to facilitate deeper emotional understanding and equip individuals with the necessary tools to navigate their feelings effectively.

Professional help plays a pivotal role in recognizing and regulating emotions. Experts can provide insights into the nuances of emotional responses, helping individuals distinguish between different feelings and their underlying causes. This understanding is crucial for developing emotional intelligence, as it allows individuals to identify triggers and patterns in their emotional reactions. By working with a professional, individuals can learn to articulate their emotions better, fostering improved communication and empathy in their relationships.

Another significant aspect of seeking professional help is the cultivation of self-compassion. Many individuals struggle with negative self-talk and harsh self-judgment, which can hinder emotional growth. Therapists can guide clients in reframing their internal dialogues and adopting a more compassionate perspective toward themselves. This shift not only enhances emotional intelligence but also promotes resilience, enabling individuals to face challenges with a healthier mindset and a greater sense of self-worth.

Knowing when and how to reach out for help is a critical skill in the realm of emotional intelligence. It requires self-awareness and courage to recognize when personal efforts are insufficient to manage emotional difficulties. Professionals can guide individuals in developing this discernment, helping them to understand that seeking assistance is a strength rather than a weakness. This guidance is particularly important in building a robust support system, as therapists often provide strategies for connecting with others who can offer emotional support.

Accessing mental health resources is essential for ongoing emotional development. Beyond individual therapy, professionals can facilitate connections to community resources, support groups, and workshops focused on emotional intelligence. These resources not only provide additional learning opportunities but also create environments where individuals can practice their skills in real-life situations. By leveraging professional help, individuals enhance their emotional intelligence, leading to improved mental health and a more fulfilling life.

Chapter 9: Practicing Self-Care for the Modern Mind

Defining Self-Care in Today's World

Defining self-care in today's world requires a comprehensive understanding of its multifaceted nature, particularly as it pertains to mental health. Self-care encompasses a range of practices and strategies aimed at enhancing well-being and managing stress. In an era marked by rapid technological advances and social connectivity, self-care has evolved beyond simple relaxation techniques to include proactive measures for emotional and mental health. It is essential to recognize that self-care is not merely a luxury but a necessary component of maintaining mental wellness, especially in the face of modern life's challenges.

At its core, self-care involves recognizing and responding to one's own needs. This means developing emotional intelligence, which allows individuals to identify their feelings and understand how these emotions influence thoughts and behaviors. By practicing emotional awareness, individuals can make informed decisions about when to engage in self-care activities such as meditation, journaling, or time management. These techniques are not only effective for alleviating stress but also play a crucial role in fostering resilience and promoting a balanced lifestyle.

In today's fast-paced environment, the importance of time management cannot be overstated. People often find themselves overwhelmed by responsibilities and expectations, leading to burnout. Effective time management strategies can help individuals prioritize tasks, allocate time for self-care, and create a structured approach to their daily lives. By carving out time for personal reflection and relaxation, individuals can enhance their productivity and emotional well-being. This conscious approach to managing time contributes significantly to one's overall mental health.

Self-compassion is another vital aspect of modern self-care. It involves treating oneself with kindness and understanding in times of difficulty, rather than engaging in self-criticism. Acknowledging that everyone experiences struggles fosters a sense of connection and reduces feelings of isolation. When individuals practice self-compassion, they are more likely to recognize when they need help and to reach out for support. This willingness to seek assistance is crucial, as it allows individuals to access mental health resources and build a supportive network.

Defining self-care in today's world means embracing a holistic view of mental health that incorporates practical techniques, emotional intelligence, and community support. As individuals become more aware of their needs and develop effective self-care practices, they empower themselves to navigate life's challenges with greater resilience. By prioritizing mental health and well-being, individuals can cultivate a more balanced and fulfilling life, illustrating the profound impact of self-care on the modern mind.

Self-Care Practices for Emotional Well-Being

Self-care practices for emotional well-being are essential components of maintaining a balanced mental state in today's fast-paced world. Engaging in regular self-care not only enhances emotional resilience but also fosters a greater understanding of one's feelings and thoughts. Techniques such as meditation, journaling, and effective time management play pivotal roles in cultivating emotional intelligence. These practices help individuals recognize their emotional triggers, control their responses, and develop a deeper awareness of their mental health.

Meditation serves as a powerful tool for emotional regulation. By dedicating time each day to mindfulness meditation, individuals can create a space for introspection, allowing them to observe their thoughts and feelings without judgment. This practice encourages a calm and centered state of mind, which is crucial when faced with emotional challenges. As people become more adept at meditating, they often find themselves better equipped to handle stressors, leading to improved emotional stability and clarity.

Journaling is another effective self-care practice that promotes emotional well-being. Writing down thoughts and feelings can provide an outlet for expression and reflection, enabling individuals to process their emotions more thoroughly. This practice encourages self-discovery and can help identify patterns in behavior and emotional responses. By regularly documenting experiences and feelings, individuals can track their emotional evolution over time, fostering a deeper understanding of their mental health journey and highlighting areas that may require additional attention or support.

Time management is also crucial in the context of self-care, as it directly influences the ability to engage in activities that promote emotional well-being. Establishing a structured routine that prioritizes self-care activities can help mitigate feelings of overwhelm and stress. By allocating specific times for relaxation, exercise, or socialization, individuals can ensure that they make room for self-care amidst their daily responsibilities. This proactive approach not only reduces anxiety but also reinforces the importance of valuing one's emotional health as a priority.

Recognizing when to reach out for help is a vital aspect of self-care. Understanding that seeking support from friends, family, or mental health professionals is not a sign of weakness but rather a courageous step towards emotional well-being is crucial. Building a reliable support system fosters resilience and provides individuals with the resources they need to navigate challenging emotions. Accessing mental health resources, whether through community programs, online platforms, or professional counseling, can further enhance one's emotional toolkit, ensuring that individuals are equipped to manage their mental health proactively and effectively.

Creating a Sustainable Self-Care Routine

Creating a sustainable self-care routine is essential for enhancing mental health and promoting overall well-being. A self-care routine should be tailored to individual needs and preferences, ensuring that it is both enjoyable and feasible. To start, individuals should reflect on their current lifestyle, identifying stressors and areas that require attention. This process may involve journaling to articulate thoughts and feelings, which can help clarify what specific self-care practices may be most beneficial. By acknowledging the challenges one faces, it becomes easier to design a routine that addresses these issues while incorporating activities that bring joy and relaxation.

Incorporating techniques such as meditation can significantly enhance a self-care routine. Meditation promotes mindfulness, enabling individuals to become more aware of their thoughts and emotions. Practicing mindfulness can help reduce stress and anxiety, making it easier to navigate daily challenges. Setting aside even a few minutes each day for meditation can foster a deeper connection with oneself, allowing for greater emotional intelligence. As individuals become more attuned to their emotional landscape, they can better recognize their feelings and learn to respond to them with compassion rather than reactivity.

Time management plays a crucial role in establishing a sustainable self-care routine. It is essential to allocate time for self-care just as one would for work or other commitments. This can involve creating a weekly schedule that prioritizes self-care activities, ensuring they are not overlooked amidst life's demands. Strategies such as setting specific goals, breaking tasks into manageable steps, and establishing boundaries can help maintain a balance between responsibilities and personal well-being. By consciously carving out time for self-care, individuals reinforce its importance in their lives, making it a non-negotiable part of their routine.

Practicing self-compassion is another vital element in nurturing a sustainable self-care routine. It is important to acknowledge that everyone experiences difficulties and setbacks. Embracing this mindset allows individuals to treat themselves with kindness during challenging times. When faced with stress or failure, practicing self-compassion can mitigate feelings of guilt or shame, fostering a more positive self-image. This practice encourages individuals to reach out for help when needed, reinforcing the importance of seeking support and accessing mental health resources. Understanding that seeking help is a sign of strength can empower individuals to take proactive steps in their mental health journey.

Building a support system is essential for sustaining self-care practices. Surrounding oneself with supportive friends, family, or mental health professionals can provide encouragement and accountability. Engaging in group activities, such as support groups or classes focused on self-care techniques, can enhance motivation and create a sense of community. Sharing experiences with others can also foster emotional intelligence, as individuals learn from each other's perspectives and coping strategies. Establishing a robust support network is a critical component of a sustainable self-care routine, ensuring that individuals have the resources and encouragement they need to prioritize their mental health continually.

Chapter 10: Integrating Emotional Intelligence into Daily Life

Daily Practices to Enhance Emotional Intelligence

Daily practices that enhance emotional intelligence can significantly contribute to mental health and self-care routines. Emotional intelligence involves recognizing, understanding, and managing our own emotions while also being attuned to the emotions of others. To cultivate this essential skill, individuals can incorporate specific daily activities that foster awareness and emotional regulation. These practices not only improve interpersonal relationships but also empower individuals to better navigate their emotional landscapes.

One effective practice is mindfulness meditation, which encourages individuals to focus on the present moment without judgment. By dedicating a few minutes each day to mindfulness, individuals can develop a greater awareness of their thoughts and feelings. This heightened awareness allows for better recognition of emotional triggers, enabling individuals to respond thoughtfully rather than react impulsively. Engaging in mindfulness can also reduce stress, improve concentration, and enhance overall emotional well-being.

Journaling is another powerful tool for enhancing emotional intelligence. Allocating time each day to write about feelings, thoughts, and experiences can provide valuable insights into one's emotional patterns. Reflecting on daily events and the emotions they evoke fosters a deeper understanding of oneself. Additionally, journaling can serve as an emotional release, helping to process complex feelings and reducing anxiety. By regularly recording and reflecting on emotional experiences, individuals can identify recurring themes and learn how to manage their emotions more effectively.

Practicing self-compassion is crucial for developing emotional intelligence. This involves treating oneself with kindness and understanding during difficult times, rather than engaging in self-criticism. Daily affirmations or moments of self-reflection can reinforce a compassionate mindset. By acknowledging that everyone experiences challenges and setbacks, individuals can cultivate resilience and emotional balance. This self-compassionate approach encourages a healthier relationship with oneself, promoting a more positive emotional state.

Building a strong support system is vital for enhancing emotional intelligence. Regularly reaching out to friends, family, or support groups creates a network of understanding and empathy. Engaging in open conversations about emotions can help normalize feelings and foster connections. Whether through casual check-ins or deeper discussions, sharing experiences with others allows for mutual growth and understanding. Additionally, knowing when to seek professional help is an important aspect of self-care. Accessing mental health resources, such as therapy or counseling, can provide further support in navigating emotional challenges and developing emotional intelligence.

Setting Goals for Emotional Growth

Setting goals for emotional growth is an essential aspect of self-care and mental health awareness. These goals can help individuals identify areas for improvement in their emotional intelligence, enabling them to better recognize and control their emotions. By establishing clear, achievable goals, one can create a structured path toward emotional resilience and well-being. This process begins with self-reflection, where individuals assess their current emotional state, identify triggers, and understand their emotional responses. Through this introspection, it becomes easier to set specific goals that align with personal aspirations for emotional health.

One effective way to set goals for emotional growth is to apply the SMART criteria: Specific, Measurable, Achievable, Relevant, and Time-bound. For instance, instead of stating a vague goal like "I want to be more emotionally intelligent," a more specific goal would be "I will practice mindfulness meditation for ten minutes each day to improve my awareness of my emotions." This approach allows for progress to be tracked and adjustments to be made as needed. By following the SMART framework, individuals can create a roadmap that enhances their emotional skills over time.

In addition to setting SMART goals, it is crucial to incorporate techniques that support emotional growth. Journaling, for example, serves as a powerful tool for processing emotions and reflecting on experiences. Individuals can set a goal to journal regularly, focusing on their feelings related to specific events or challenges. This practice not only aids in emotional regulation but also fosters self-compassion by encouraging individuals to examine their experiences without judgment. Furthermore, incorporating mindfulness practices or engaging in supportive communities can provide the necessary encouragement and accountability for achieving emotional growth goals.

Another important aspect of goal-setting for emotional growth is recognizing when and how to reach out for help. Setting a goal to connect with a mental health professional or join a support group can be instrumental in fostering emotional resilience. These resources offer valuable insights and coping strategies that can enhance one's emotional intelligence. Additionally, having a strong support system composed of friends, family, or community members can significantly contribute to achieving emotional growth objectives. Establishing relationships with those who understand and support one's emotional journey is vital for maintaining motivation and accountability.

Setting goals for emotional growth is an ongoing journey that requires commitment and flexibility. As individuals progress, they may find that their initial goals evolve or change based on new insights and experiences. Embracing this fluidity allows for continued personal development and deeper emotional awareness. By prioritizing emotional growth through intentional goal-setting and incorporating supportive practices, individuals can cultivate a more resilient and fulfilling emotional landscape, leading to improved mental health and overall well-being.

Long-Term Benefits of Emotional Intelligence on Mental Health

Emotional intelligence (EI) plays a pivotal role in fostering long-term mental health benefits. At its core, emotional intelligence involves the ability to recognize, understand, and manage one's own emotions, as well as the emotions of others. This skill set not only enhances interpersonal relationships but also contributes significantly to self-awareness and self-regulation. Individuals who cultivate emotional intelligence are more adept at navigating life's challenges, leading to reduced stress and anxiety levels. Over time, these benefits accumulate, creating a solid foundation for mental well-being and resilience.

One of the primary long-term benefits of emotional intelligence is improved stress management. People with high emotional intelligence are better equipped to identify stressors and respond to them in a constructive manner. By recognizing their emotional triggers, they can employ techniques such as meditation and journaling to process their feelings. This proactive approach reduces the chances of emotional overload and burnout. Furthermore, the ability to articulate emotions clearly fosters healthier communication within personal and professional relationships, which can alleviate stress and contribute to a more supportive environment.

Emotional intelligence also enhances the practice of self-compassion, a crucial element in maintaining mental health. Individuals with high EI are more likely to treat themselves with kindness during difficult times, recognizing that imperfection is a part of the human experience. This self-compassion diminishes negative self-talk and self-criticism, which are often detrimental to mental health. By fostering a nurturing inner dialogue, individuals can cultivate a more positive outlook on life, leading to increased resilience against mental health challenges such as depression and anxiety.

In addition to these personal benefits, emotional intelligence plays a vital role in establishing and maintaining a robust support system. Those who recognize the importance of emotional connections are more inclined to seek help when needed and to offer support to others. This reciprocal relationship creates a network of understanding and empathy, which is essential for navigating the complexities of mental health. Individuals who can express their emotions and needs are more likely to access mental health resources and find community support, further reinforcing their mental wellness.

The long-term benefits of emotional intelligence extend to overall life satisfaction and fulfillment. By understanding and managing emotions effectively, individuals can set realistic goals, maintain motivation, and pursue meaningful relationships. Emotional intelligence encourages a proactive approach to life challenges, allowing individuals to embrace change and uncertainty with confidence. As a result, those who invest in developing their emotional intelligence not only enhance their mental health but also enrich their overall life experience, creating a cycle of positive growth and well-being.

Resources

Here are some valuable resources for mental health support, including helplines, apps, books, and medical journals:

Hotlines and Helplines

1. National Suicide Prevention Lifeline: 1-800-273-TALK (1-800-273-8255)
- Offers 24/7 free and confidential support for people in distress, prevention, and crisis resources.
2. Crisis Text Line: Text "HELLO" to 741741
- Provides free, 24/7 text support for individuals in crisis, connecting them with trained crisis counselors.
3. SAMHSA's National Helpline: 1-800-662-HELP (1-800-662-4357)
- A confidential and free resource for individuals seeking treatment for mental health or substance abuse issues.

Mental Health Apps

1. Headspace: A meditation and mindfulness app offering guided meditations and courses to help reduce stress and improve mental clarity.
2. Calm: An app focused on meditation, sleep, and relaxation techniques to promote mental well-being.
3. Moodfit: A comprehensive mental health app that allows users to track moods, set goals, and access resources for managing mental health.
4. Sanvello: Provides tools for managing stress, anxiety, and depression, including guided meditations and mood tracking.

Books

1. "The Body Keeps the Score" by Bessel van der Kolk
- Explores the connection between trauma and physical health, providing insights into healing and self-care.
2. "Self-Compassion: The Proven Power of Being Kind to Yourself" by Kristin Neff
- Offers strategies for developing self-compassion, which can enhance emotional resilience and overall mental health.
3. "The Gifts of Imperfection" by Brené Brown
- Encourages readers to embrace their imperfections and cultivate a sense of worthiness and self-acceptance.
4. "Feeling Good: The New Mood Therapy" by David D. Burns

- A practical guide that offers cognitive behavioral therapy techniques for managing negative thoughts and improving mood.

Medical Journals

1. Journal of Clinical Psychology
- Publishes research and articles on clinical psychology, including studies on mental health interventions and therapies.
2. American Journal of Psychiatry
- A leading journal that covers the latest research on psychiatric treatments, mental health trends, and clinical practices.
3. Psychological Bulletin
- Offers comprehensive reviews of research in psychology, including topics related to mental health and well-being.
4. Journal of Mental Health
- Focuses on issues related to mental health, providing research articles and reviews on clinical practices, policies, and patient experiences.

These resources can provide valuable support and information for readers seeking to enhance their mental health and well-being.

Dear Readers,

As I reflect on the journey of writing Mental Health 101: Self-Care for the Modern Mind, I am filled with gratitude for each of you. Thank you for choosing to embark on this journey with me, for your courage in prioritizing your mental health, and for opening your hearts and minds to the possibilities of self-care.

In a world that often demands more than we can give, it can be challenging to put ourselves first. Your willingness to engage with these concepts and strategies is a testament to your strength and resilience. I hope this book has provided you with valuable tools to recognize your feelings, manage stress, and cultivate a deeper understanding of yourself. Remember, it's perfectly okay to seek support and take time for yourself; you are deserving of both.

I believe in the power of self-care and emotional well-being, and I trust that you will continue to invest in your mental health journey. As you move forward, may you embrace your unique path with kindness, compassion, and curiosity. You are not alone; a supportive community is waiting for you, and the journey to mental wellness is a shared one.

Thank you for being part of this book and for believing in the importance of mental health. I am inspired by your courage, and I look forward to hearing about your progress and successes. Remember, you are stronger than you realize, and every step you take toward self-care is a step toward a brighter future.

With heartfelt appreciation,

Monica Lynne Chase

www.ingramcontent.com/pod-product-compliance
Lightning Source LLC
Chambersburg PA
CBHW080051270726
48653CB00045B/3902